All Scripture references taken from the KJV of the
Holy Bible, unless otherwise indicated.

marlenemilestheauthor.com

Freshwater Press, USA

ISBN: 978-1-960150-66-0

Paperback Version

CONTENTS

From the Back

God, Kingdom Spouses
You, and Kingdom Friends

Freshwater Press

Introduction

In this book we will talk about God, the Face of God, You, Kingdom friends as well as Kingdom spouses.

There is so much talk about kingdom marriages and kingdom spouses nowadays, that I wanted to address some things that the Lord has shared with me.

There is a message on YouTube that this is based on, Behind His Back, and I found it to be a very moving message, but this book has so much more.

Thank you for reading this book, may you be enlightened, and changed.

Dr. Marlene Miles

The Face of God

No man, in the flesh, has seen the face of God and lived, but the idea of God's face being turned toward us, looking on us gives us comfort, assurance, peace and quiet, or exuberant joy.

> When thou saidst seek ye my face, my heart said unto thee,
>
> Thy face, Lord, will I seek. (Psalm 27:8)

We should be looking for the face of God.

There's the blessing also from the Old Testament:

The Lord lift up his countenance upon thee and give thee peace, (Num 6:26).

As it is used here, *countenance* is the face of God. It means that God is looking on us with favor and with approval.

We love the face of God. We love to think that God's face is turned to us and that His countenance is looking upon us. And we love it when God is doing nice things for us. We love it when He is doing things for us such as creating the heavens and the Earth, preparing the amazing place that He's given us to live. Thank You, Lord.

The Lord also has given us great provision, precious promises and gifts. God is thorough and He gives us everything that pertains to life and to godliness.

We like it when we know that God is hearing us, looking upon us and answering us. To think God is watching over us, noticing us, looking at us, blessing us – it's very satisfying, unless we are sinning and trying to hide something, or like Adam and Eve, completely hiding from God.

You may have heard me say before, but it bears repeating that the Word of God has to endure and go through extreme warfare to get to man, all the time. So, the sinner who is hiding is also hiding from the *Word* of God which is what is able to save him and keep his soul and body out of hell.

In the cool of the day God visited Adam & Eve, the Word was right there with them, but like Jerusalem where Jesus walked among them, Adam & Eve also *missed it.* Jerusalem missed the presence of God, the very face of God. Adam and Eve who had *known* the face of God, hid from it.

A person has to be deceived and pretty demonized to hide from that Goodness. Unless guilty, as I said before, the presence of God is terror to demons who hide or try to hide from God, as the legions of demons did to Jesus in the Gadarenes. We are made of the same stuff as God, we should gravitate to God like magnets. Demons are the opposite; this is why they hide or try to hide from God.

Yes, surmise that people who run from God are usually demonized and are not ready or planning to repent. This doesn't mean that everyone who talks about God isn't a hypocrite or Pharisee. We must discern every spirit.

While we love the face of God—you think that's something, wait until you see Him from the back. God is so awesome that even the back of Him is glorious.

And the Lord said unto Moses, I will do this thing also that thou hast spoken, But thou has found grace in my sight, and I know thee by name. And he said I would seek to show me thy glory. And he said, "I will make all my goodness pass before thee, and I will proclaim the name of the Lord before thee. And I will be gracious to whom I will be gracious, and I will show mercy on whom I will show mercy. And he said, Thou canst not see my face, but there shall no man see me and live. And the Lord said, Behold, there's a place by me. And thou shalt stand upon a rock, and it shall come to pass while my glory passes by, that I will put thee in a cleft of the rock and will cover thee with my hand while I pass by. And I will take away my hand, and thou shalt see my back parts, but my face shall not be seen.

Moses said, *Lord, show me Your glory.* If God is going to show us His glory, He must show us His Wisdom and Knowledge. He shows us His justice, His loving kindness, His Mercy, His Holiness, His wrath. His patience, His long-suffering, His goodness, His largesse. His Omnipotence, Omniscience, His Omnipresence. God must show all of these attributes in order to show us His glory, but there is so much more to God. He must show us His magnificence, His warmth, His beauty, strength, and loveliness along with His perfection and His grandeur.

When we look at all of God's creation, the stars and the heavens, we must say how great God is. The whole Earth, which is full of His glory, testifies.

The human eye cannot look directly on the glory of God, but we can look on the works of His hands--, and live. We can attest to the beauty and the marvel of nature, and of all mankind. But we cannot directly, in our human flesh and with human eyes look at the glory of God and live. We can't fathom the full glory of God.

Those who don't believe that God is real should have their God-given eyes looked at because all they have to do is look around and see. They didn't create any of this world or universe any more than you and I created *ourselves*.

God--, Jesus is not only the *cause* of the bright and morning star, but He IS also the Bright and Morning Star. He's the Rose of Sharon. He's altogether lovely. He's full of glory.

The Holy Spirit speaks of the Lord and the Father over and again, saying,

The heavens declare the glory of God. The skies proclaim the work of His hands day and night. Day after day they pour forth speech. Night after night they display knowledge. There's no speech or language where their voice is not heard.
Psalm 19:1-6

We're supposed to be like Jesus. And God intends that man should show the glory that God has put on man as well. There's a glory that man carries. There's glory on you. And it should be just as Moses saw when God passed by that cleft of the rock, Moses saw glory. There should be a glory on you that when you pass by or when you leave a place, or a room, (for example) people may say, *Wow, that was wonderful, what he or she shared. That really blessed me,* or *That helped me.* They should not be able to stop themselves from saying something good about you.

Not, *"I'm so glad they finally left, because I was so tired of them."*

Even if they don't say anything, they should either feel something, or sense something. They can sense that something changed either in the room, in the situation, or in themselves. Either physically, soulishly --, at least, or their spirit man quickened – even if just a little. And the change should be good. That's glory.

If you are not a sinner, hey – even if you are a sinner, you might like God from the front. Humans love to ask God for stuff. Humans love to ask anybody for things. Humans love to be served. Even when they should be grown or growing up, they want to sit in a highchair and be served. They want to do adult stuff with only the responsibility and accountability of a child. That is the hallmark of an unprospered soul.

Look at the glory that follows God. Look at what is at the back of God. What follows you is a strong indication of who you are. Signs and wonders follow God. They could follow you, too, if you are a carrier of His Word and His Spirit. At the very least, and as promised, Goodness & Mercy should follow you; that is part of the glory that follows a man.

Anybody can step to you and while looking right at you, they can fake it. They can pretend. They can be cheesing at you, grinning, smiling, winking--, but is that the real them? If you are not discerning, spiritually, you may believe that fake, flesh façade.

One's glory, which is seen from the back, *after* they've left the room, after some time has passed, could be why the human head cannot turn all the way around to the back. *What it is, is what it is.* You can't fake it with a toothy grin.

Without prosthetics or plastic surgery, never in the history of time has anyone ever been able to fool anyone with their back.

The Essence of You

The essence of you is not what you're putting on, it's what you just *are*. So, you've got friends who love to see your face, right? They love it when you're walking toward them, bearing gifts, bringing goodness and attention with plans to spend time with them. They smile in your face, too, but as soon as you turn your back what are they saying about you? What are they saying about you when you're not there? What are they saying when your back is turned? What they are saying behind your back is based on their perception of your front and also the essence of who you are.

Women, that man who is so glad to see you and you are the only person in the absolute world when you two are together, he loves your face, and other things about you. But when he doesn't call you, text you, take your call, or take your text after you two are not in the same room together, that's a sign of how he sees your glory.

He doesn't.

He doesn't see you as having glory. You are an object, something to do. When your back is turned, and you don't hear from him and can't find him, in his eyes you have no worth, you have no glory.

In this case, you could have been faking glory, or he could have been faking that you had glory, or that he could *see*--, or recognize your glory.

Guys like that are hunting for flesh. The Word of God says that no flesh shall glory in His presence. Ladies, putting your flesh on parade will not show anyone, or cause anyone to see your **glory**. Go ahead, put those away. Lower your skirt hem length and you should not need a pharmacy prescription because your pants are too tight. There is no real or lasting glory in that, although the carnal man glorifies flesh--, mutating, changing, rotting flesh--, all the time.

God says no flesh shall glory in His presence. Yet, the carnal man glorifies the opposite of what God glorifies and cares nothing for the real things of God. That's devil-work, and that man is devil-led.

They Smile In Your Face

The old R&B song says, *They smile in your face, but all the time they want to take your place, the backstabbers*. I say, if you're a child of God, even if *they* don't SAY anything good about you, they may sense it. They may know it. And knowing it may make them feel some kind of way. Hopefully it's a good way, but it may not be, depending on who you are and depending on who *they* are. You could be great and what you just imparted was great, but they may be a jealous soul, a hater. They may be resentful that YOU came up with that great idea, at work, for example, or maybe an amazing new invention, and not them. Now you're getting attention, favor, accolades from man. Your glory is evident, now.

They may even take it further and be angry toward God because God gave that idea to YOU and not them. When, all the while all they had to do is develop their relationship with God and let the Holy Spirit develop them and their character, so God could put some GLORY on them.

An undeveloped character cannot carry glory. It would be too much for them. God's got **real glory**, so the devil has false glory or fake glory. God doesn't sell glory.

Fake or temporary glory, the *appearance* of glory, the devil's glory is for sale. Anything from the devil costs **everything** and none of us have enough money, things, or stuff to redeem ourselves if we get into a devil deal. We need Jesus Christ to get out of any evil covenant. We need the Holy Spirit to realize if we've gotten into a devil deal. We need the Word of God to stay out of devil deals, even for false glory.

I'm not trying to give anyone a complex here, this is not about inciting paranoia, but it is a real question. What do you think people say about you, think about you, feel about you when you are *not* in their company? That is an indication of the glory that is on you, their ability to see it, or their willingness to admit that you have God's grace and glory on you.

What do we say about God when we don't think God is listening, looking on us and His ears are attuned to us? Do not be among the numbers of people who curse God when things are not going their way. For all you know what is happening to you, that you may not even like is going God's way as He is pruning reproving, teaching, growing, developing and refining you.

Fire burns. But God's Fire is certainly more merciful than hell's fire. The Lord's refining flame is a gentle Mercy compared to the unrelenting inferno of hell that will never stop burning either hell itself of the souls damned to it for Eternity.

What do we think about God? Do we think He's fair or unfair? Reasonable, or unreasonable? What thoughts go through our own heads? Is God requiring too much of me? Or can you say, *"I love the Lord."* Can you say, *"He is the light of my life, He is the reason I am vertical and walking this Earth right now"*?

Is there praise and worship to the Lord from you, unsolicited? Is there unsolicited praise, where no one is standing on a stage or in front of you with a microphone to **MAKE** you, beg you, or drag you into worship?

Can't Touch That

As Moses saw the glory of God go by, there's nothing negative Moses could have ever said about God. We all have hope and optimism when we see the face of God, but when we see His back and He hasn't done for us, or we think He hasn't done for us what we've asked. What are we saying *then*? Where is our faith *then*?

When the Israelites, at the base of the mountain thought God wasn't looking, they fell into idolatry, like, big time. On the mountain, Moses was getting to know God by seeing His glory. Down the mountain, or in the valley, the rest of the group thought that God was gone because God did not show up on *their* schedule.

Man has a problem with time. Recently I have met a lot of grown people who do not know how to tell time. No, they really don't. I don't mean on an analog clock versus a digital clock, I mean they do not understand time and how it works. Flying from Point A to Point B, a young lady said, *It only takes 4 hours to get there.* I was amazed and surprised. So, out of curiosity, I looked at the flight online myself. She had said, *"We leave at midnight and get there at 4am."*

No, that's not it at all. The flight leaves one time zone at midnight and arrives at another destination, in a different time zone at 4am. In the original time zone it is 6am. The flight takes 6 hours.

God is not boxed in by time, especially by people who can't even tell time, or understand time. God is not boxed in by anything, really. So when God was on the mountain with Moses, being Omnipresent, He was also down the mountain with the idolatrous hoard that was sinning and committing *whoredoms*. The problem is that without the Holy Spirit, you won't know that. You won't know what time it is in God.

All the stuff we are asking God for, God's already done ALL of that. **All of it.**

(Read my book, **Living for the NOW of God**.)

The Glory Comes After

The glory and the essence of the thing comes *after* it. After. It's when the tale is told, they say. The tale is told *after.* In time we can judge a thing. We can judge if a thing is real or if it wasn't real. If the thing is good or bad we will know about it in time, that is. After that time has passed, we can evaluate that situation to see what that was. Was that real or false? You've heard people say, *Well at first, I thought it was great but then things changed.* Or, they may say, *When we first met it was amazing, but then later on, not so much.*

The glory comes after, but humans, in their relationships have a honeymoon phase at the beginning, and without really working at the relationship and staying together may not ever get to the part of the relationship where the Glory is. The glory comes *after*.

The glory comes after; the glory of a woman the Bible says is her long hair. The hair comes after.

The glory of a cake is the icing, in my opinion, and the icing comes *after* the cake is made. Man is created in the image and likeness of God, crowned with glory and honor, but man's true glory will come *after* he is developed and conforms into the image and likeness of Christ.

Notice how we celebrate people and their accomplishments and their achievements. Not before; we celebrate them *after*. The couple that stayed together, raised a family and built a legacy will be celebrated in their golden years; the glory comes *after*.

After any man or woman has lived their life, upright before the Lord, fulfilled purpose and reached destiny, God will reward with crowns and honor. God rewards a man with an exceeding weight of glory. This glory is greater than that man realized in Earth; this is that exceeding weight of glory of which the Bible speaks.

The glory of God is all around Him, but it also follows after. God is enveloped in glory, and He is the Spirit of Glory. But the glory of God that we can look on, that we can fathom, comes *after*.

Humans, especially those who can't tell time want the glory FIRST. Then, they want to decide what that glory is worth to them, if anything, as if God is a dude in a market to bargain and bicker with. This is the epitome of ignorance and disrespect of God.

Putting On

We all have friends, and we know that people put on their best behavior-- *at first* as in relationships and families, even in friendships and marriage. Our best behavior lasts but so long; the real person has to show up at some time. The real person will show up sooner or later because *time will tell it all.* Since time tells all, we will see the glory, the true essence later because it comes *after*. The glory comes after, and the story comes after.

The test of a true friendship sometimes takes time, and it may take months or years to really get to know somebody and their complexities. *You* might be that complex person who's just going along to get along and not letting your true self be known until you feel that you can trust your comrades, acquaintances, your associates. It may take some time to make them into friends. You might be that complex person who takes time to get to know.

Time will tell because the story comes after, and the glory comes after. How you feel about a person sometimes is not known until they've left the room. And at that time, you may start to consider your feelings. Maybe at that time you're able to take the time to actually *feel*, whereas you may not have been able to feel in real time when the person was there, either because you were enamored of them, impressed by them, on guard, afraid of them, or showing off for them. Or maybe you repressed your whole personality because that (human) person was in the room.

There have been times when I've wondered why people can't do simple things that they **know** how to do--, even in church. Are they *putting on* too much – are they working on appearing, seeming, or *being holy* so much that they forget how to walk, chew gum, or any other simple thing that should be automatic or at least easy for them to do?

Any of us could be guilty of deferential behavior toward higher-ups or objects of our affections from time to time. Maybe you wanted something from them, so you wanted to present yourself in a certain way to them. But now that they've left the room, now you can consider the mood, the experience, the atmosphere of that room. What does it feel like? Is it heavy or is it uplifting? Is it hopeless or is it hopeful?

How do you know that your spouse doesn't feel like this sometimes when they get home and evaluate the atmosphere of your home? –without *realizing* that they are evaluating the atmosphere of the home, or anywhere else. It's automatic. Discernment at whatever level you have discernment, is automatic.

Does your spouse have to push through just to get into the house? Is it difficult to come home? Are you difficult, emotionally frustrating, or unpleasant to come home *to*? Is the atmosphere in the home *of God*? Is there a heavy glory cloud in the house, or is the atmosphere demonic or chaotic? Is there a storm or trouble brewing? Is it gonna be a bad night?

How do *you* feel when your spouse gets home? I'll confess that when I heard the garage door go up, I would get a bit unsettled when my Ex was coming home. What mood would he be in? When dealing with mercurial people that is always a concern. Unless your spirit man is strong, you can be swayed to feel their negative *feels* with them, and that's usually not good for either of you, the relationship or the family.

What atmosphere do you set for your home when you are entertaining or having guests? What you invite and entertain is what lingers there.

Topic for another day: what *spirits* do you allow in your home, either in person, through devices such as TV and online, as well as through your phone? Your complaining girlfriend does not need to drop that vibe into your home every day, especially if she's not going to pray or do anything about her problems.

YOU must control the atmosphere in your own home.

Is It Safe?

How do you *feel* about the atmosphere that's in the room? What was said? What was talked about, what was done? What went on? You have a right to judge that.

If you are on a potential battlefield you can't take too long to discern if the person that you're looking at is a friend, an adversary, an opponent, or a Goliath.

If you're living in a certain situation, you must evaluate if it is *safe* to be there, to live there. You must evaluate if it is safe and healthy for you to be in that situation.

Evaluate both the physical dwelling place, and the relationships in that place. It can't take too long, but by the same token you cannot jump to conclusions. It takes discernment, prayer, careful consideration, Wisdom, and a certain speed. It takes prayer and the Holy Spirit, else, how will you see all you need to see?

How can you see spiritually until you can **see** *spiritually*? By the Holy Spirit, is how. Prayer.

Your Glory

We really don't want God to leave a place, because when God leaves, the glory of God leaves. We don't ever want *Ichabod* to be written across the door of our homes, our businesses, our families, our dwelling places, or our lives.

God's glory is so amazing. It's got its own weight. It's heavy. Without spiritual muscles, without your spirit man being built up, even the glory that's intended for man will not – cannot be carried, (properly). It is heavy.

God's glory filled the Tabernacle; the anointing of it was so heavy that the priest couldn't minister. (1 Kings 8:11, 2 Chronicles 5:14). This is why people fall down in services; the anointing has glory with it and it has weight.

The heaviness of God's glory was so much that the people couldn't stand under it. If somebody tells you that you're a lightweight and they are not talking about your physical weight, they may be saying more than you think. They are talking about your verve, your *heart*, whether you are courageous or forthright or not. Without glory, we're all lightweights tossed about with any wind of doctrine. Sometimes I wonder, if we are on Earth, in the cleft of this third rock from the sun, to witness the Glory of God?

This is about Jesus, the Mighty Rock, the Rock that is higher than I.

Yes, we can see the glory of God from right here in the cleft of this rock--, while on the planet, but also while we are hidden in Christ Jesus, Our Rock.

Oh Lord, listen to my prayer. From the ends of the Earth I call to you. As my heart grows faint, lead me to the Rock that is higher than I, (Psalm 62:20)

We serve the only living God. So God, who is Omnipresent is present all the time by His Spirit and He is always ministering to us. Always.

In the year that King Uzziah died, I saw also the Lord sitting upon the throne high and lifted up, and his train filled the temple. Isaiah 6:1

In the year that King Uzziah died, Isaiah said he saw the Lord sitting upon the throne high and lifted up.

Above it stood the Seraphim. Each one had six wings. With twain he covered his face, and with twain he covered his feet and with twain he did fly. And one cried out to another. And said Holy, Holy, Holy is the Lord of Host. The whole earth is full of his glory. And the post of the door moved at the voice of him that cried, and the house was filled with smoke. All earth is filled with God's glory. (Isaiah 6).

So the glory of the Lord fills the whole Earth, and it fills the heavens. The whole Earth, Lord is filled with Your glory.

There are some people who come into a room and just about suck the air out of it. But God *is* the air in the room. He is the life. He is the joy. He is the Only Living God. He's the Wisdom in every room. He is the sweet-smelling aroma. God is Spirit and He is Life. He shows forth glory wherever He goes, and He is all glorious. He's enveloped and enrobed in glory. So much glory that even glory comes after Him.

The glory of the Lord filled the temple like the train of a majestic garment. And when you carry the presence of God at your own level, that's the result that you should have, too--, at your level. When the life of God is in you, is the room filled with Wisdom when you are there? Is it filled with mercy? Kindness? Goodness?

Yes, I asked you about your friends, because the company you keep says a lot about you. And now I ask you about you. What is the atmosphere like when *you* leave a place? What follows after you? What *spirit* do you leave in the air when you go through or leave a place? Or what *spirit*, or *spirits* might I ask? Not bitterness, not jealousy, not pettiness, right?

Shouldn't you leave the essence of the Spirit of God, **at your level**, when you go through a room, or leave a room? Shouldn't something favorable linger with the person you were just with, after you've gone, until they see you again?

Do people say things to you such as, *"I was just thinking about you the other day and remembered something you said to me"*? It was something that ministered to them or something that blessed them or nurtured their soul, or grew their spirit. That's glory.

You don't want to be so obnoxious or ungodly that people would say, *Oh no, it's them again. I'm not gonna answer the phone, don't open the door no matter how much they ring the bell. Just pretend we're not here.*

The train of the Lord, due to all His glory, filled the temple.

In your wake after you leave a place, is there glory? There is a glory that's due man. There's a glory that man carries.

Goodness and Mercy should follow that man.

Goodness and mercy shall follow me all the days of my life, (Psalm 23:6).

Who and what in the natural follows you says a lot about who you are. Please don't have evil and pestilence following after you. Not anxiety, or pettiness, nor vexation. No, none of that. You should have goodness and Mercy and Truth and Grace following after you.

Godly followers, both spiritual and natural, are an indication of the type of glory on a man. And you know that when a person leaves a room, it's what's said about them that tells his real reputation. What people really think of him indicates his real glory, or the lack of glory. We want to have some of that glory, a good name, a good reputation, *don't we*?

A good name is rather to be chosen than choice silver and fine gold, (Proverbs 22:1)

Look for the amazing teaching and book on satanic glory cover by Anthony O. Akerele. He breaks it down so we can know how a person's glory is covered and the disastrous results of it being covered and also how to get it uncovered. Sin is the chief culprit in a person's glory being covered.

There's a cost to glory, there are disciplines needed to have a good reputation. Coming through afflictions work out glory in us.

The glory of God should surround you and envelope you as well. It should follow you. And it should be something that people notice. It should be something that people remember, something they talk about even after you've left their presence.

Whether they're two-faced or not, people should be saying good things about you after you've left. They should not be able to help themselves. Even if they are two-faced, they **must** say something good about you. Because **the thing that's good about you is God about you**. Goodness and Mercy should be following after you all the days of your life. Amen.

After Jesus

And behold, a woman which was diseased
with an issue of blood 12 years came
behind him and touched the hem of his
garment. For she said within herself, if I
may but touch his garment, I shall be
made whole. But Jesus turned him about,
and when he saw her, he said, Daughter,
be of good comfort. Thy faith have made
thee whole, and the woman was made
whole from that hour, (Matthew 9:20-)

I mention here from the New
Testament that the hem, that is the fringe,

tassel, or border (fringe, phylactery) of Jesus' garment could heal. That's how much glory was in Him. That's how much glory filled Jesus. He exuded power and glory. The hem of His garment healed the woman with the issue of blood. That should make sense since the anointing flows from the head and the Old Testament tells us of the anointing flowing down in Psalm 133:1.

Yet Jesus was ever telling people that He healed, *Don't tell anybody.* But they couldn't help it. They would say, *Come and see a man.* They couldn't help but tell of His Glory. Because Jesus came to Earth also to personify the glory of God.

Peter's shadow could heal. Paul's handkerchiefs could heal. These are part of the **glory** that a man can carry. But it's the glory of God ultimately that creates and bestows this glory on man. Man has no inherent glory of his own; *God* crowned man with Glory and honor.

Glory and honor, reputation, name, are the things that follow after a person. If the shadow of a man can heal, what must his countenance be like? What must the ministry of his face be like?

May the Lord make His countenance shine upon you.

Shouldn't the glory you got from God, the glory that's due man--, shouldn't it heal something? Help something? Help someone, do something? Change something, change somebody?

Can you change somebody's life? Can your presence change a situation? A room? A person?

Crowned With Glory

What WEIGHT of glory are you carrying? Heavy is the crown on the head of the king. We are *little k* kings on Earth. What is the weight of the crown of glory that is on your head?

God rewards according to our good works, in Eternity. Prophetically what your crown may look like is according to your good works here and now. Resisting the works of the flesh, evangelism, forgiving 70X7, staying humble, one-another ministry, not gossiping and sowing discord are all hard work, but with help of the Holy Spirit we prosper our souls to where God allows us the glory that is due man.

The Devil's Behind

The Book of the Revelation reads that the devil with his tail took a third part of the *stars* from the sky.

...and his tail drew the third part of the stars of heaven and it cast them to the earth. (Revelations 12:4)

The devil, as he was cast out and fell from Heaven, took the third part of the angels with him, so the devil's hinder parts is his pointy tail, as he is often depicted.

Jesus' garment could heal. God's train fills the temple with glory, so the people cannot stand, the priests cannot minister.

But with the back of the devil with his tail, he steals and corrupts angels.

So who do you want to serve? Again? *Who*?

That should not even have to be a question.

Be The Best

As we are going through this life with our friends, our fake friends, former friends, our exes, and other complicated relationships, there is still an eternal weight of glory for us. The turmoil that we sometimes have to endure in our complex relationships is what is *working* this glory in us. If God can use a thing, He will allow it. As bad as some of the stuff we go through is, most often it is of our own making, through sin, rebellion, disobedience, or ignorance. God does not want you to be a perpetual victim, but you should be quicker to blame yourself than to blame, accuse, be mad at, or walk away from God.

So, our shadow, our garment, our handkerchief, anything that has touched, been connected to or come into contact with us, or our essence, should be imbued with the glory that is on us. Even as we pass by, stop by or spend time with folks, our shadow, touch, handkerchiefs or garments should minister to people. We exude essence; there should be some glory in our essence. It was the case for Jesus and He is our supermodel.

Maybe when we hug, touch, with intention, or the person hugging or touching us has intention and we'll feel virtue come from us, as Jesus did with the woman with the issue of blood. Maybe we won't actually feel anything leave us. It'll just *be*.

There's an eternal weight of glory that is beyond comparison. What we go through on Earth is only a light affliction compared to the glory that awaits us. We must keep focused on the things of God as we go through life.

To the negative, items that you've had, worn, or touched--, even the dirt from under your shoe or your tire print can represent you on evil altars. Your blood, sweat, tears, DNA, skin cells, hair fingernails, toe jam is not known to heal anyone, Biblically speaking, but it certainly has been used for evil.

Even more to the negative, there is an evil touch, an evil handshake, there can be an evil transfer of *spirits* that we must stay prayed up and guarded against. There is a transference with tangible objects and substances that we should not allow to happen to us. Most often those types of transfers are made by sin.

Without this lengthy conversation, God says, Don't sin. Don't fornicate. Don't commit adultery. Don't masturbate. Don't look on other people's nakedness (pornography). Shouldn't we just do what we are told by God? The one who doesn't know anything is about 1 year old. The one who has to be told the same thing over and over again is 2 years old. The one who always has to ask *why*, spiritually, is 3 years old. *Why? Why? Why?*

I say all that to say, why aren't we transferring Goodness and Mercy, and love, joy and peace when we touch people, with intention.

Life goes by quickly, people. We may not know all of what will be tomorrow. Maybe life is like a vapor that vanishes suddenly. We should spend our years wisely, growing and growing up spiritually.

We must endeavor to be the best that we can be even while we are going *through*. Be the best friend. Be the best person, the best spouse, the best family person, the best parent. And even in times of adversity, we rise above and we grow spiritually. We prosper in our souls and in our relationship with Christ and with people. In order to carry God's glory, in order to carry the glory that is due to man, and to be a blessing to others, we must rise above.

We do the will of God. We do the work of Him Who sent us. We do it while it is day. Because many are the afflictions of the righteous, but the Lord will deliver us out of them all. So our present troubles are small, really, in the grand scheme of things. They won't last long, but they produce in us a glory that vastly outweighs all that we could think.

The trials of life will increase our relationship with God and our faith in God as long as we don't blame Him and run away. They'll increase our prayer life. They'll drive us sometimes to our knees, to prayer. They will drive you to victory.

Be A Friend

We need to be *Kingdom people--,* easily recognized as such. There is no need to even use discernment to try the Spirit that is running your life when you are a Kingdom person. It should be obvious by your fruit, the Fruit of the Spirit that you are a Son of God.

In our lives, we need to be Kingdom friends. You need to be a Kingdom boss or a Kingdom employee, depending on what position you find yourself. You need to be a Kingdom sister, a Kingdom brother--, or better yet, be a friend, because a friend loves at all times, while a brother is born for times of adversity.

Kingdom Spouse

Some are Kingdom wives and Kingdom husbands. Some are *looking* for Kingdom spouses. You want a Kingdom spouse? Then be a Kingdom friend. Start there. You want to *be* a Kingdom spouse? Be a Kingdom friend first.

You ultimately will be friends with your Kingdom spouse first anyway. Learn how to be that first so you don't marry your enemy. **Be a friend; marry your friend**.

You will need glory for a successful marriage. Glory fosters love and respect in relationships. If your spouse does not esteem you, that is not conducive to a good marriage.

All these promotions and glory that come from the Lord will be entrusted to you. God entrusted all of us to carry His glory, at what level depends on us--, our relationship with Him and others and the condition of our heart. If we're Kingdom people we've got love and we also need soul prosperity so we carry it well, not letting it go to our head. That's so when we actually have real glory, the glory that is due man, we don't spin around and from the back pull a third part of anything, any part of humanity, with us--, like the devil.

People aren't to follow *us*, they're to follow God.

The Holy Spirit leads us into all truth and <u>always</u> points us back to Jesus. We, too should always be pointing back to Jesus Christ, our Lord and Savior.

In Him we move and breathe, and we have being. In Him is healing and blessing, and peace and joy. In Him, we will also be followed all of our lives by Goodness and Mercy.

In Him is where the glory is. We are not touching God's glory. We admire it; we see it. We worship God in His Majesty. Amen. But God's glory is **His**. God's glory is so glorious that even behind His back He's glorious. And Jesus, from the back is fully engrossed and enveloped in God, so much so that the hem of His garment healed.

And what's at *your* back?

What's At Your Back?

What fragrance or funk are you leaving in your wake? Goodness and Mercy should be following you for the sake of the people behind you. We do not scorch the Earth or God's people in it.

God is gracious, and He puts us here with free will, kind of on our own recognizance to do as we see fit. Women of God, if you are seeking a Kingdom spouse, don't pervert this. God's essence and glory should be what people notice when you leave a room or leave a building, not just your physical attributes.

Dress to Impress

What are you wearing? Who put that garment on you? Trust this, the clothes you're wearing will manifest the thing that <u>matches those outfits</u>.

If you're not wearing a proper Kingdom garment, you will not manifest a kingdom's spouse. Well, yeah, that outfit may be able to get you a husband for the night. It can get you a husband, a carnal, flesh-minded husband. Because you're actually dressing for the *spirit(s)* that is in you. The outfit that you wear will attract the same *spirits* that are in the men you encounter. That is how your attire will attract **more** of the same *spirit(s)* that's in you. Birds of a feather. You've heard it said that most often you attract what you <u>are</u>, not what you want. It's that essence again – can't hide it, can't dress it up, can't trick folk – most of the time. Some criminals and evil agents are very adept at this kind of trickery. The Bible says that the devil can turn himself into an angel of light and that even the very elect of God could be deceived, were it possible.

That's where your prayers and come in. Stay prayed up , say and believe it is not possible, in the Name of Jesus.

Now you want a Kingdom husband, or man if you're looking for a Kingdom wife, what are your potential mates like when you're looking at them face to face? And when they leave your presence, what are they like? What do you remember? What do you recall about them? *What is their glory, looking from the back?*

Keep It Real

Ladies, you've been on a date and it was wonderful. It was glorious. He treated you like you were the only person in the room; he couldn't take his eyes off you. **Men do that, you know.** You two were in your own little microcosm and there were no other people in the world. He even got irritated when the waiter came over as if the waiter was a demonic invader. Each of you even turned off your phone, flipped them upside down on the table, or had them in airplane mode.

But you weren't on a plane, you were on a date. And he encouraged you to *be yourself,* say whatever you wanted to say, talk about whatever you wanted to talk about, and he was so attentive, all ears.

This date was so fantastic. It lasted for hours, even into the night. Were there drinks? There shouldn't have been. You became so elated you were delirious or nearly so; you felt like you were floating on a cloud.

If what happened next was censored, I will respect that in this book, but *that* shouldn't have happened, either.

Oh, but you *feel* he is "the one" and you two will be together **forever** because you want it to be that way and he behaved or acted as if that was the way it should be or already was. You feel he is Mr. Right, and he's trying to convince you that he is Mr. Right Now, but he hasn't told you that.

Did you pray about this date before or after you went on it? *After?* Yes, ask God if there was any glory in this date, or this person.

You finally met someone who *sees* you, who hears you, who appreciates you. This is fantastic. You're in love!

Tomorrow. No call. No text.

The next day, nothing.

The third day; radio silence.

This is a war zone and the war is in your mind. Where is he? What is he doing? Why hasn't he called? Why hasn't he answered my calls? My texts? *Is he okay?*

Baby, he's fine. He's on to his next thing.

But I thought he loved me, liked me, wanted me, was interested in me.

Yeah--, *that night.*

This man is letting you know, as he runs away at sunrise or whenever he ran away from you and went to hide under whatever rock he hid under, that you either have no glory, he sees no glory on you, or that he is unable to see or appreciate *glory*.

Further, the sin(s) you committed with him dimmed whatever glory you did have. It didn't just dim your glory in his eyes, in the physical, but in the spirit as well. **A notification has gone out in the spirit that you are now "damaged goods" evidenced by your lackluster or non-existent glory.**

Even if you were all glorious at the beginning of that date your glory has been dented, damaged, or completely destroyed by the time his demons got through with you. Worse, ALL the glory that he either saw or feigned to see, he <u>**TOOK**</u>. He stole ALL your virtues, all the goodness that he saw or could take out of you. *Very Grinchy.*

Now that your glory is covered, or **GONE**, it's not just you hesitating to meet someone new and possibly get to know them, it's that you're not even going to be as attractive as you were to normal and appropriate people. The covered glory mark on you has downgraded you to what you *will* be attractive to until you get your glory back--, if you *ever* get your glory back. Here's your new list:

- Old guys.
- Married guys.
- Broke guys.
- Creepy guys.
- Immature guys.
- Dumb guys.
- Unsaved guys/heathens.

You've been defiled and now you're in the bargain basement.

You need Jesus. Because of where you are now, and because YOU didn't see that *he* had **no glory** in the first place. Women, his "potential" is NOT glory.

You both need Jesus. He needs Jesus because he never had Jesus in the first place. He was just running his flesh game.

Women: the bad boys are so good at things they shouldn't be doing, namely sex because they have a *demonic assist*, whether they know it or not. It's ungodly, and those demons--, his demons are highly trained, experienced, and *transferrable*. A man with no spiritual covering or protection should not be an option for dating. Let him meet the Lord and get saved, first. The glory will come *after* that.

As far as *your* glory goes, he doesn't know he took it, unless he is an experienced satanic agent and knows it. Unless he's dumb, he should know he took your dignity, honor and self-respect. If he's not a willing devil agent, all he knows is he's gotta have it and convenient for him, you're the one he's with – tonight. His demons that he doesn't even know he has and will surely deny having, are running the show. Whatever power his demons are working under, that's who either now *has* your glory or covered it.

Tell yourself: I got this thing and it's golden. It is called glory. God gave it to me and God won't take it away from me, but people want it, or they don't want me to have it – or both. There are ways to keep it, and there are ways to lose it. I've got to know both. In this book, I've outlined a few of the ways to keep it and the ways to lose it, but let's just say SIN is the surest way to lose your glory.

This is not just about relationships and marriages, your glory determines your entire life: FAVOR, opportunities, education, career, money and finances, health, success and even children. You need to maintain your glory!

Kingdom Marriage

The kingdom marriage is a covenanted union between a man and a woman. And they promise to function as *one* under divine authority for God's purposes while answering both their individual calls and their joint calling. Yes, many are called to be the help mate, but women have callings too.

A kingdom marriage is ordained; it's sanctioned by God. And I like to believe that the two people who are marrying each other are two people who are *supposed* to be married to each other. They are fulfilling God's plan and purpose for their lives. And also the life of their children. Amen.

Kingdom Husbands are under God's leadership and submit to the Lordship of Jesus Christ and the Holy Spirit. He is changed day by day into the image of Christ. We're all changed from glory to glory, from Grace to Grace. Amen.

Kingdom marriage is something we all say we want. There's a whole lot of talk about this now. A Kingdom spouse and a marriage is not something you *apply for* or register to win in the Kingdom. You're *called* to it.

First, a couple must work on being friends. Friends with others, yes, but NOT friends with benefits; that is a worldly construct. You need to be *agape* friends with the person you want to be your Kingdom spouse. The Bible speaks of friends in many passages. Friends bought the paralytic man to Jesus, in the Gospel of

Mark. Those are true friends who cared about the person's well-being and they helped him even when he was down and out. That is a friend. Friends look out for friends.

Jesus said, *This is my commandment, that you love one another as I have loved you. No one has greater love than this to lay down one's own life for his friends.*

And he says you are my friends if you do what I command, (John 15:14).

Kingdom Friends

There were friends all through the Bible. David and Jonathan, the three friends of Daniel, Shadrach, Meshach, and Abednego. Job had friends. Yeah, they had some of their own false ways of thinking. Some of the stuff they told Job may not have been on point, but Job didn't throw them to the curb, Job was a friend, and when Job prayed for his friends, God delivered Job. Amen.

Christian friends are not selfish. They don't just use friends to meet their own needs. Christian friends are trusted confidants. Friends are trusted with other people's personal business sometimes.

You need to pray for the *spirit of counsel* to come upon you. So when you hear the counsel of another person, or the problems, the woes, or the concerns of a friend, you don't repeat it. The *spirit of counsel* is what you need.

The Witchcraft of Gossip

Gossip is witchcraft. When you gossip, you're saying what *you* see, what *you* think and what *you* expect over a person's life--, not necessarily what God says. That is *blind witchcraft*. It is destructive. It is sinful. Christian friends should have confidence that their private struggles will be kept between friends and not spread all over the planet. The glory of the Lord fills the Earth--, not gossip.

A perverse man, sows strife and a whisperer, separates the best of friends. A violent man entices his neighbor and leads him in a way that is not good. (Proverbs 16:28).

King James version says that a forward man's soweth strife and a whisperer separated chief friends, entices his neighbor. Leads him into the way. That's not good.

Wealth makes many friends, for the poor is separated from his friends,

(Proverbs 19:4).

John the Apostle was a friend of the Lord. You see, a godly friend speaks truth into your life. Even when it's difficult to hear, they speak the truth in love.

A real friend sticks closer than a brother,

(Proverbs 18:24).

Jesus had many disciples and apostles. He had best friends, such as Peter, James and John.

Are you a friend? Do you show yourself friendly? That is how you begin to make friends. No, you shouldn't feel like a victim or feel rejected, but is the back of you saying anything?

We are created in God's image and likeness. If the back side of God is exuding glory and telling of His gloriousness, we should be something like that too.

What is the back of you saying? Anything? What do you look like or sound like, from the back? You know the back of you-- after your friend has shared their problems and their woes with you, and then when they turned *their* back, or you turn your back, what is the back of you saying? What can we expect to hear? Are you praying for them? Are you interceding? Or, are you talking about them? What's the back of you saying? Is there any *glory* in the back of you? Is there Goodness? Is there Mercy? Is there intercession and prayer?

Or when you turn your back on your friend, is it as though you don't have any friends at all, or that you're not really a friend? Are you compassionate and merciful? Do you keep your promises to your friends?

In all relationships, there may be takers and givers. But if you are a friend, be a Kingdom friend. If not, evaluate your reasons for being connected to any person. If you're not their friend or can't be their friend, let that connection go. They deserve a friend. They deserve good friends. If you can't be one, let the connection go.

We all deserve real friends. Find them or ask the Lord to find them for you. And especially, I say, if you want a Kingdom spouse. You need to be a Kingdom **friend**. Take that away from this message. Because you will be friends with your spouse.

Jesus said, according to John 15:15. *Henceforth I call you not servants, for the servant knoweth not what is Lord do with that I have called you friends. All things that I've heard of my Father I have made known unto you.*

A friend talks about God to his friends. A friend celebrates the Lord. A friend helps his friend grow up in the things of the Lord because of all that truth in Love. You will do that with your Kingdom spouse as well. It's not all about the party and floaty, ethereal dates.

And when your beloved is overwhelmed that you call him or her *friend* that is the mark of the Kingdom friend, and if it's appropriate, you are on your way to becoming a Kingdom spouse.

Perfect and true pure in all your ways.
Oh, Lord, there's nothing else like you.
No one like you. And all these things keep

me in all of you. And I'm overwhelmed.
That you would call me friend.

Fred Hammond

The glory of God that's supposed to rest on you should be such that when you leave home for the day to go to work or to the grocery store, that Goodness and Mercy that you left in your wake with your Kingdom friend should bring them comfort or assurance, or peace, or joy. That's the beauty of God; the anointing knows what you need and brings you that very thing. That glory, that ministry, is still *alive* even when you've left the building; even when you've left your spouse's eyes and ears--, their presence.

People hold you in esteem and respect you when you show divine traits. Under normal conditions and circumstances, it is the divine that is loved in every loved one. When you show people

Wisdom, lovingkindness, and Mercy they see that as love and care toward them. When you show people that you walk upright before the Lord, unless they are demonized, they respect that. When you show justice and mercy, patience, long-suffering, goodness all in balance, people see that as glorious.

Ladies, telling a man that you are a good girl, a good church girl and getting busy with him AT ALL, and especially on the first date is the absolute worst thing you can do for your glory, your dignity, your reputation and GOD's reputation. That man now thinks you are the biggest liar in the world, and he basically was out to prove that anyway, especially if he is not a Believer, or you suspect he's not.

Oh, you are worried that you may lose him if you don't sleep with him? THEN HE AIN'T THE ONE! He's not the one for a Kingdom marriage. Your glory, in his eyes, goes to ZERO. I'm not saying that people don't have "chemistry" and if you marry a person because both of you are all lusted up – people do it every day. That is *not* a Kingdom marriage and it usually lasts about 2 years. Maybe in that time you both could get saved and God can transform your marriage into a Kingdom marriage where both your glories can shine.

Sorry – back on subject –

Not being a know-it-all, but not being an ignoramus will be seen by normal people as glory. Any of these displays which are like God, similar to God, or following after the manifestations of God make **you** look glorious What GLORY do you leave in your absence, in your wake? It depends on if you are walking in or working with any of the aforementioned attributes.

Because everything that God has is alive, everything that He gives us is alive. God doesn't even ride on anything dead. God's ride, His *car* is Cherubim. He rides on a living thing. God doesn't play with dead things, old things, inanimate objects and dead idols. Dead things cannot produce fruit. So, if you are alive in Christ, what you produce is also alive, so even when you leave the building, your fruit remains.

Single ladies, as for your dating life, if God doesn't deal with dead things – things inanimate and/or spiritually dead, why would you even talk to or go out with a *spiritually dead man*? The spiritually dead have NO glory. If you connect with him, he will either try to take your glory or resent you for having it.

Prayers

Father, thank You that I'm redeemed by Christ Jesus, redeemed for Your glory and Your honor. I am Your workmanship created in Your image, for good works.

Fire of the Holy Spirit and purifying power of the Blood of Jesus, cleanse me now; make me whole. Make my life fit for Your glory, in Jesus' Name.

Lord, let me carry the glory and the Grace that You planned for me from the foundation of the world, in Jesus' Name.

Father, baptize me afresh with the Holy Spirit of Promise, Your Holy Spirit, the Spirit of Glory, in the Name of Jesus.

Lord, let me not grieve the Holy Spirit as I go through this process.

Lord, I declare that my star and my light is shining so bright before men (mankind) that they will see Your good work in my life.

Father, even as I pass by--, if not the hem of my garment, if not my handkerchief, if not my shadow, let the glory of the essence of who I am in You *minister*, in Jesus' Name.

Thank You, Lord, for this *spirit of boldness* and *courage* to act on the glory that You put in my spirit, in the Name of Jesus.

Lord, correct and protect those things that concern me by Your Mercy, because Your Mercy endures forever. Forsake not the work of Your own hands.

And Lord, I ask to be in health, so let my soul prosper. Thank You, Lord.

I decree and declare that I'm walking in power, walking in miracles and favor, in Jesus' Name.

The Word declares that I'm a priest and a royal priesthood and a *king* to You. Lord, thank You.

Lord, help me to be a better friend. Make me a better friend to my friends, Make me a *Kingdom* friend. And Lord, make me a better spouse.

If I'm already married, let me be a Kingdom spouse who is in a Kingdom marriage. Or let me not miss my Kingdom partner if I am not married as ordained by God, in the Name of Jesus.

God give me Wisdom and understanding to pick the right partner, in Jesus' Name.

Lord, deliver me from every temptation that I may encounter in trying to get a spouse. Do not let me be duped or do stupid things, instead give me knowledge and Wisdom, in the Name of Jesus.

Lord, I repent for every type of sexual sin that I have committed, in Jesus' Name.

Remove from me the garments of reproach and the garments of shame and dishonor, in the Name of Jesus.

Spiritually Lord, anything that you didn't put on me, I curse the evil exchange. I send every evil garment back to sender and I require that the original garment that You gave me for my life be returned and placed on me, in Jesus Name.

I demand the return and/or uncovering of my glory, in Jesus' Name.

In the Name of Jesus, I command and change every negative verdict of the enemy against me to my good and to bless me, according to Your Word, Father God.

In the Name of Jesus, Holy Ghost, destroy and roast to ashes every evil weapon of the enemy against my courtship, engagement, wedding, marriage, and married life, in the Name of Jesus.

I destroy every organized program of the enemy against me to miss my Kingdom friends or destiny helpers, and marital partner in life, by the Blood of Jesus, in the Name of Jesus.

Lord, provide all finances for my wedding and marriage, for a successful happy marriage, in the Name of Jesus. I reject, cancel and destroy every root of poverty, making it difficult for me to marry and stay happily married, in the Name of Jesus.

Holy Ghost, lift every delay hindering Mr. or Miss Right from reaching me, in the Name of Jesus.

Holy Ghost Fire roll off every marital problem placed on me by the devil, in the Name of Jesus.

Lord, stop every enemy action against my life, including evil human persecutors, in Jesus' Name.

I cover myself and my life with the Blood of Jesus.

Lord, manifest beauty in my life, in the Name of Jesus.

Lord, thank You for beauty for ashes, in the Name of Jesus.

Spirits of rejection and *reproach,* working against me. I bind you, and I cast you into the pit from where there is no return, in Jesus Name.

Any anti-marriage steps taken against me, roast by Fire, in the Name of Jesus.

Every evil companion, counselor, fake friend, fake minister or fake pastor that is robbing me of opportunities to meet and marry the right partner, be gone from my life today, in the Name of Jesus.

Every plan of the enemy against me and my divine destiny, and every monitoring *spirit*, I roast by Fire, in the Name of Jesus.

Every evil *spirit* that is causing me not to get married I cancel your plans, in the Name of Jesus.

Every evil arrow shot at me, I gather you all together, dip you in the Blood of Jesus and return to sender, in Jesus' Name.

Lord, I bind star hunters and all other evil agents in the Earth trying to stop me from fulfilling my destiny, in the Name of Jesus.

Every evil covenant I've made with people, mermaid, or animal *spirits*, I cancel those covenants, now by the Blood of Jesus.

I also cancel all unfulfilled vows and covenants that I've made with former partners, or their families that is now working against me, in the Name of Jesus.

Father Lord, expose secrets of the enemies of my life and destroy them, in the Name of Jesus.

Lord, make me better for Kingdom relationships, Kingdom friendships and for Kingdom marriage, in the Name of Jesus. Lord, make me ready for Kingdom marriage and for my Kingdom spouse, in the Name of Jesus.

Holy Ghost, arrest every enemy that's after my life and throw them into a prison that has no key. Throw them into the prison that they prepared for me, in the Name of Jesus.

Lord, let there be a permanent halt on any *spirit of disunity* between me and my spouse, or intended, in the Name of Jesus.

Lord, send my right partner that will enable me to reach spiritual destiny and enjoy maximum marital satisfaction, in Jesus' Name.

Lord, give me special Grace and Favor from my in-laws, in the Name of Jesus.

Marriage crashers, all anti-marriage powers against me, die, in Jesus' Name.

Every ancient gate or door blocking my blessings, your strongman must die, in the Name of Jesus.

Every consequence of parental mistake made against my life, die, in Jesus' Name.

Every blockage my parents had in meeting, dating, getting married, having children, and staying married, I command you to stop working against me today, in the Name of Jesus.

Every mark of failure in my life, the Blood of Jesus blots you out, in Jesus' Name.

Serpent of darkness, issued against my marriage, die.

Marital failure in my life, die, in Jesus' Name.

Power of delay, release your vise from around my life, in the Name of Jesus.

My marriage, my Kingdom marriage, appear by Fire and let enemies be put to shame, in the Name of Jesus. Amen.

Thank You, Lord. Thank You Father, for hearing and answering prayers. I bind all retaliatory *spirits*, *powers* and *principalities*, from attempting payback at me for these prayers, in the Name of Jesus.

I seal these declarations in every realm, age, timeline and dimension, past, present and future, to infinity, in the Name of Jesus Christ. Amen & Amen.

Dear Reader

Thank you for buying and reading this book. I pray that it has enlightened and strengthened you.

May the Lord break you out of every captivity and may He restore you *at least* sevenfold, all that you have lost and all that has been taken from you--, your glory, your virtues, even ***time,*** as He restores the years.

In the Name of Jesus,

Amen.

Dr. Marlene Miles

Other books by this author:

AK: The Adventures of the Agape Kid

AMONG SOME THIEVES

Ancestral Powers

Blindsided: *Has the Old Man Bewitched You?*

Churchzilla, T*he Wanna-Be, Supposed-to-be Bride of Christ*

Demons Hate Questions

Devil Weapons: Unforgiveness, Bitterness,...

Dream Defilement

Don't Refuse Me, Lord (4 book series)

Evil Touch

Fantasy Spirit Spouse

FAT Demons (The): *Breaking Demonic Curses*

The Fold (4 book series)

    The Fold (Book 1)

    Name Your Seed (Book 2)

    The Poor Attitudes of Money 3

Do Not Orphan Your Seed

From the Back: God, Kingdom Spouses, You & Kingdom Friends

got HEALING? Verses for Life

got LOVE? Verses for Life

got HOPE? Verses for Life

got money?

How to Dental Assist

How to Dental Assist 2

Let Me Have A Dollar's Worth

Living for the NOW of God

Lose My Location

Man Safari, *The*

Marriage Ed. *Rules of Engagement & Marriage*

Made Perfect in Love

Motherboard (The)- soul prosperity series 1

Plantation Souls

Power Money: Nine Times the Tithe

STARSTRUCK

Upgrade: How to Get Out of Survival Mode (1)

Toxic Souls (Book 2 of series)

Legacy (Book 3 of series)

Warfare Prayer Against Beauty Curses

Warfare Prayer Against Poverty

When the Devourer is Rebuked

The Wilderness Romance *(3-book series)*

The Social Wilderness

The Sexual Wilderness

The Spiritual Wilderness

Journals & Devotionals by this author:

The Cool of the Day – for times with God

He Hears Us, Prayer Journal in 4 colors

I Have A Star, Dream Journal kids, teen, adult

I Have A Star, Guided Prayer Journal, Boy, Girl

J'ai une Etoile, Journal des Reves

Let Her Dream, Dream Journal multi colors

Men Shall Dream, Dream Journal, (blue or black)

My Favorite Prayers (multiple covers)

My Sowing Journal (in three colors)

Tengo una Estrella, Diario de Sueños

Illustrated children's books by this author:

Be the Lion (3-book series)

Big Dog (8-book series)

Do Not Say That to Me

Every Apple

Fluff the Clouds

I Love You All Over the World

Imma Dance

The Jump Rope

Kiss the Sun

The Masked Man

Not During a Pandemic

Push the Wind

Slide

Tangled Taffy

What If?

Wiggle, Wiggle; Giggle, Giggle

Worry About Yourself

You Did Not Say Goodbye to Me

www.ingramcontent.com/pod-product-compliance
Lightning Source LLC
Chambersburg PA
CBHW061152040426
42445CB00013B/1660